ELEGANT C  I

DUY NGUYEN & ROBERT FATHAUER

STERLING INNOVATION
An imprint of Sterling Publishing Co., Inc.

New York / London
www.sterlingpublishing.com

STERLING, the Sterling logo, STERLING INNOVATION, and the Sterling Innovation logo
are registered trademarks of Sterling Publishing Co., Inc.

2 4 6 8 10 9 7 5 3

Published by Sterling Publishing Co., Inc.
387 Park Avenue South, New York, NY 10016
© 2009 by Sterling Publishing Co., Inc.

This book is comprised of materials from the following Sterling Publishing Co., Inc. titles:
Jungle Animal Origami © 2003 by Duy Nguyen
Under the Sea Origami © 2004 by Duy Nguyen
Fantasy Origami © 2001 by Duy Nguyen
Origami Birds © 2006 by Duy Nguyen
Origami Myths & Legends © 2005 by Duy Nguyen

Original origami tessellation projects written by Robert Fathauer

Distributed in Canada by Sterling Publishing
c/o Canadian Manda Group, 165 Dufferin Street
Toronto, Ontario, Canada M6K 3H6
Distributed in the United Kingdom by GMC Distribution Services
Castle Place, 166 High Street, Lewes, East Sussex, England BN7 1XU
Distributed in Australia by Capricorn Link (Australia) Pty. Ltd.
P.O. Box 704, Windsor, NSW 2756, Australia

Printed in China 12/09

Sterling ISBN 978-1-4027-6931-3

For information about custom editions, special sales, premium and
corporate purchases, please contact Sterling Special Sales
Department at 800-805-5489 or specialsales@sterlingpublishing.com.

Select origami paper designs may be available at
Kate's Paperie, 1-800-809-9880, www.katespaperie.com.

Design by Leah Lococo Ltd

CONTENTS

INTRODUCTION TO ORIGAMI

SOME YEARS AGO, when I first began learning origami, I struggled with even the simplest folds. I would look back at the instructions given at the beginning of the book again and again, reviewing the basic folds. I also looked ahead, at the diagram showing the next step of whatever project I was folding, to see how it should look, to be certain I was following the instructions correctly. Looking ahead at the "next step," the result of a fold, is incidentally a very good way for a beginner to learn origami.

You will easily pick up this and other learning techniques as you follow the step-by-step directions given for this collection of creatures. Some are fairly easy to fold, formed from only a single square of paper. Others of these fabulous creatures may call for a good deal more time and effort, with smaller and tighter folds to add creative detail. But if you persevere, I guarantee the result will most certainly be worth it.

–DUY NGUYEN

BASIC INSTRUCTIONS

Paper: Paper used in traditional origami is thin, keeps a crease well, and folds flat. Packets of specially designed sheets, about 6 and 8 inches square (15 and 21 cm), are available in various colors. You can use plain white, solid-color, or even wrapping paper with a design only on one side and cut to size. Be aware, though, that some papers stretch slightly in length or width, which can cause folding problems, while others tear easily.

Beginners, or those concerned about getting their fingers to work tight folds, might consider using larger paper sizes. Regular paper may be too heavy to allow the many tight folds needed in creating more traditional, origami figures, with many folds, but fine for larger versions of these intriguing projects. So sit down, select some paper, and begin to fold and enjoy the wonderful art that is origami.

Glue: Use an easy-flowing but not loose paper glue. Use it sparingly; don't soak the paper. A flat toothpick makes a good applicator. Be sure to allow the glued form time to dry. Avoid stick glue, which can become overly dry and crease or damage your figure.

Technique: Fold with care. Position the paper, especially at corners, precisely and line edges up before creasing. Once you are sure of the fold, use a fingernail to make a clean, flat crease.

For more complex folds, create "construction lines." Fold and unfold, using simple mountain and valley folds, to pre-crease. This creates guidelines, and the finished fold is more likely to match the one shown in the book. Folds that look different, because the angles are slightly different, can throw you off. Don't get discouraged with your first efforts. In time, what your mind can create, your fingers can fashion.

SYMBOLS & LINES

Fold lines   valley   - - - - - - - - - - - - - - -

                 mountain   - · - · - · - · - · - · -

Cut line   +++++++++++++++++++++++++

Turn over or rotate

Fold then unfold   ←——————→

Pleat fold
(repeated folding)

Crease line   ————————————————

SQUARING OFF PAPER

1

Take a rectangular sheet of paper and valley fold
it diagonally to opposite edge.

2

Cut off excess on long side as shown.

3

Unfold, and sheet is square.

BASIC FOLDS

KITE FOLD

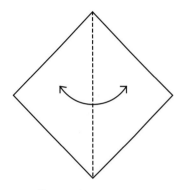

1 Fold and unfold a square diagonally, making a center crease.

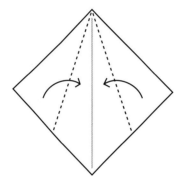

2 Fold both sides in to the center crease.

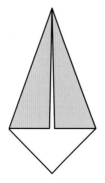

3 This is a kite form.

VALLEY FOLD

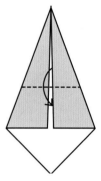

1 Here, using the kite, fold form toward you (forward), making a "valley."

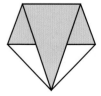

2 This fold forward is a valley fold.

MOUNTAIN FOLD

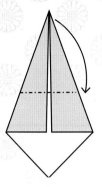

1 Here, using the kite, fold form away from you (backward), making a "mountain."

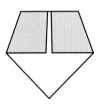

2 This fold backward is a mountain fold.

INSIDE REVERSE FOLD

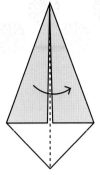

1 Starting here with a kite, valley fold kite closed.

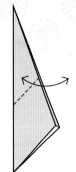

2 Valley fold as marked to crease, then unfold.

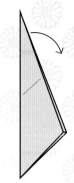

3 Pull tip in direction of arrow.

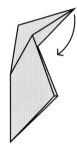

4 Appearance before completion.

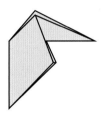

5 You've made an inside reverse fold.

OUTSIDE REVERSE FOLD

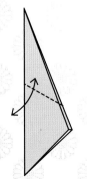

1 Using closed kite, valley fold, unfold.

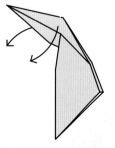

2 Fold inside out, as shown by arrows.

3 Appearance before completion.

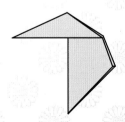

4 You've made an outside reverse fold.

PLEAT FOLD

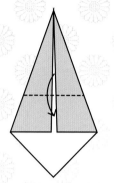

1 Here, using the kite, valley fold.

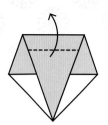

2 Valley fold back again.

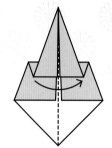

3 This is a pleat. Valley fold in half.

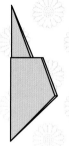

4 You've made a pleat fold.

PLEAT FOLD REVERSE

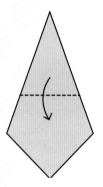

1 Here, using the kite form backwards, valley fold.

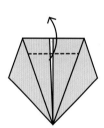

2 Valley fold back again for pleat.

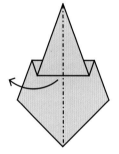

3 Mountain fold form in half.

4 This is a pleat fold reverse.

SQUASH FOLD I

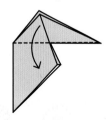

1 Using inside reverse, valley fold one side.

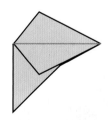

2 This is a squash fold I.

SQUASH FOLD II

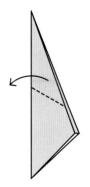

1 Using closed kite form, valley fold.

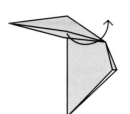

2 Open in direction of the arrow.

3 Appearance before completion.

4 You've made a squash fold II.

INSIDE CRIMP FOLD

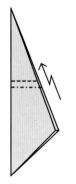

1 Here using closed kite form, pleat fold.

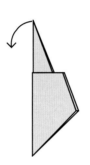

2 Pull tip in direction of the arrow.

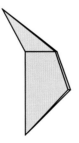

3 This is an inside crimp fold.

OUTSIDE CRIMP FOLD

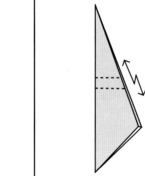

1 Here using closed kite form, pleat fold and unfold.

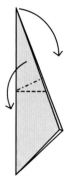

2 Fold mountain and valley as shown, both sides.

3 This is an outside crimp fold.

BASE FOLDS

Base folds are basic forms that do not in themselves produce origami, but serve as a basis, or jumping-off point, for a number of creative origami figures—some quite complex. As when beginning other crafts, learning to fold these base folds is not the most exciting part of origami. They are, however, easy to do, and will help you with your technique. They also quickly become rote. With completed base folds handy, if you want to quickly work up a form, you can select an appropriate base fold and swiftly bring a new creation to life.

BASE FOLD I

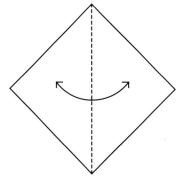

1 Fold and unfold in direction of arrow.

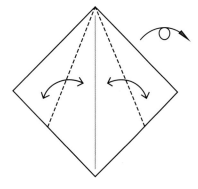

2 Fold both sides in to center crease, then unfold. Rotate.

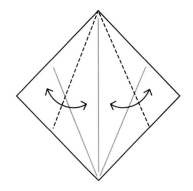

3 Fold both sides in to center crease, then unfold.

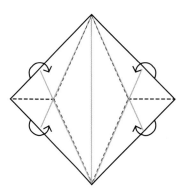

4 Pinch corners of square together and fold inward.

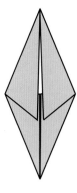

5 Completed Base Fold I.

BASE FOLD II

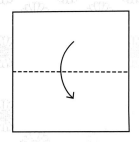

1 Valley fold.

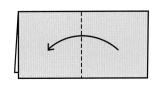

2 Valley fold.

3 Squash fold.

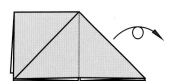

4 Turn over to other side.

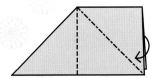

5 Squash fold.

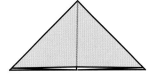

6 Completed Base Fold II.

BASE FOLD III

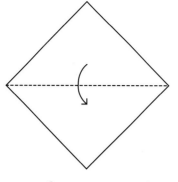

1 Valley fold.

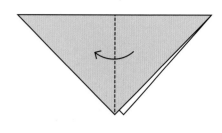

2 Valley fold.

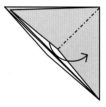

3 Squash fold.

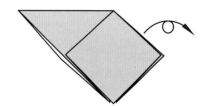

4 Turn over.

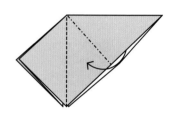

5 Squash fold.

6 Valley fold, unfold.

7 Valley folds, unfold.

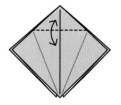

8 Valley fold, unfold.

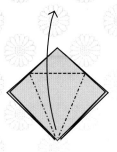

9 Pull in direction of arrow, folding inward at sides.

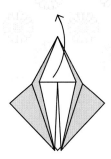

10 Appearance before completion of fold.

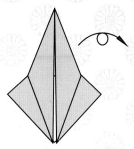

11 Fold completed. Turn over.

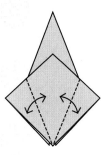

12 Valley folds, unfold.

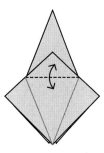

13 Valley fold, unfold.

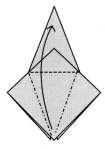

14 Repeat, again pulling in direction of arrow.

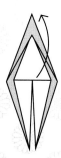

15 Appearance before completion.

16 Completed Base Fold III.

GORILLA

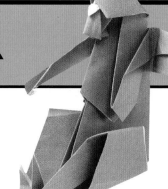

PART I

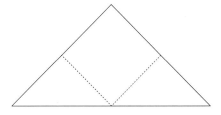

1 Start with square sheet cut diagonally, then valley fold.

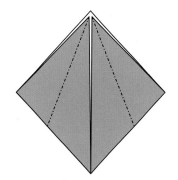

2 Inside reverse folds.

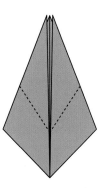

3 Valley folds.

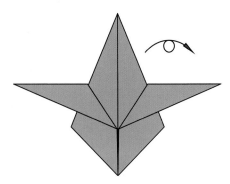

4 Turn over to other side.

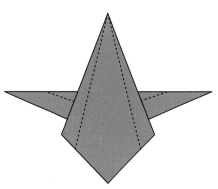

5 Valley folds and squash folds.

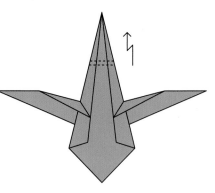

6 Pleat fold.

14

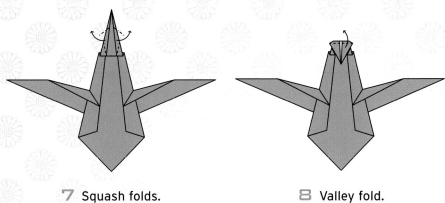

7 Squash folds.

8 Valley fold.

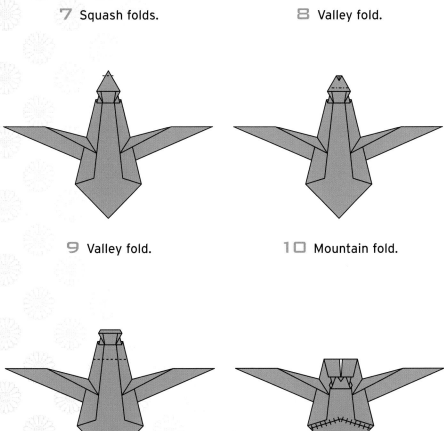

9 Valley fold.

10 Mountain fold.

11 Valley fold.

12 Cut as shown.

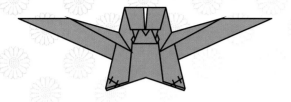

13 Cuts as shown.

14 Inside reverse folds.

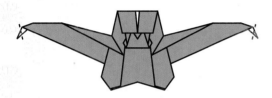

15 Outside reverse folds.

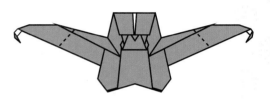

16 Valley folds.

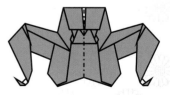

17 Mountain fold in half.

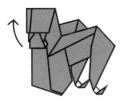

18 Pull and crimp head into position.

19 Pull and crimp open.

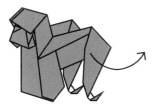

20 Unfold in direction of arrow.

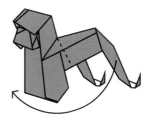

21 Valley fold both sides to extend arms.

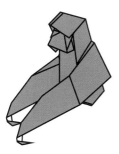

22 Completed part 1 (top) of gorilla.

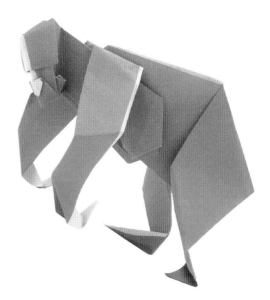

17

PART II

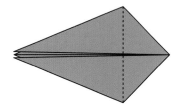

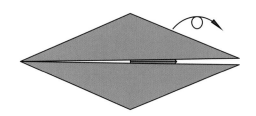

1 Start with step 3 of part 1, then valley fold.

2 Turn over to other side.

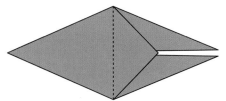

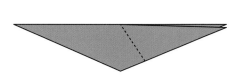

3 Valley fold.

4 Valley fold in half.

5 Valley fold both front and back.

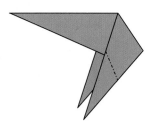

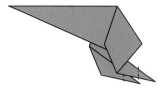

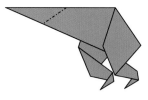

6 Mountain fold both front and back.

7 Repeat.

8 Inside reverse fold.

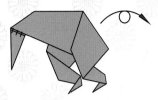

9 Cut as shown and rotate.

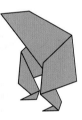

10 Completed part 2 (rear) of gorilla.

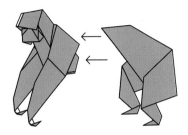

1 Join the two parts together as shown and apply glue to hold.

2 Completed Gorilla.

LION

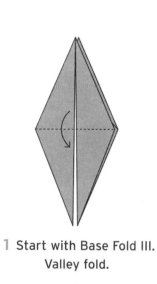

1 Start with Base Fold III.
Valley fold.

2 Cut as shown.

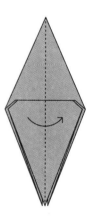

3 Valley fold.

4 Rotate.

5 Inside reverse fold.

6 Outside reverse fold.

7 Repeat.

8 Cut as shown.

9 Valley folds front and back.

10 Valley fold.

11 Make cuts to front layers.

12 Valley fold cut parts.

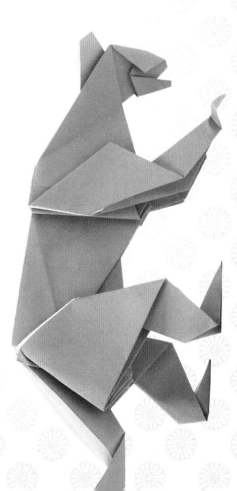

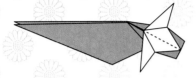

13 Valley fold back up into position.

14 Trim ears, as shown.

15 Valley folds front and back.

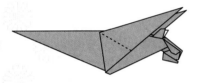

16 Valley fold both sides.

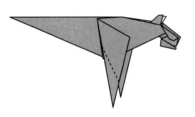

17 Mountain fold both sides.

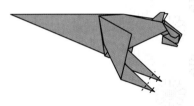

18 Valley and mountain fold each side.

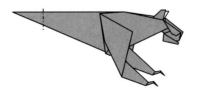

19 Inside reverse fold.

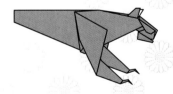

20 Completed part 1 (front) of lion.

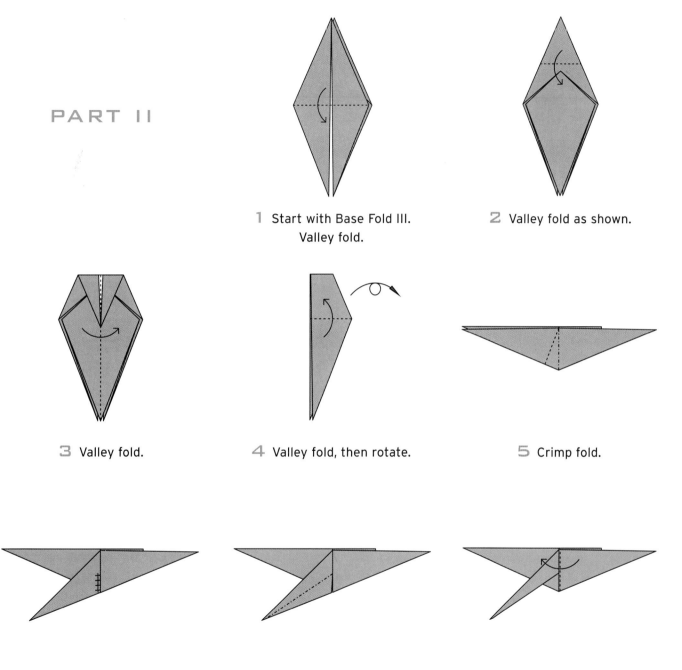

PART II

1 Start with Base Fold III.
Valley fold.

2 Valley fold as shown.

3 Valley fold.

4 Valley fold, then rotate.

5 Crimp fold.

6 Cuts as shown.

7 Mountain folds both front
and back.

8 Valley fold.

23

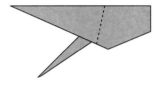

9 Valley fold.

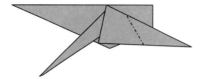

10 Inside reverse fold.

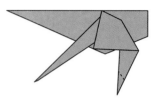

11 Inside reverse fold.

12 Turn over to other side.

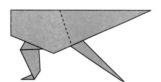

13 Valley fold.

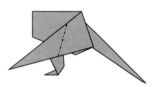

14 Inside reverse fold.

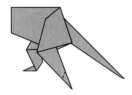

15 Repeat.

16 Valley fold.

17 Inside reverse fold.

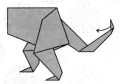

18 Valley unfold tail tip.

19 Completed part 2 (rear) of lion.

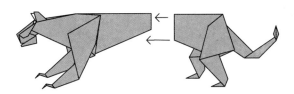

1 Join both parts together as shown and apply glue to hold.

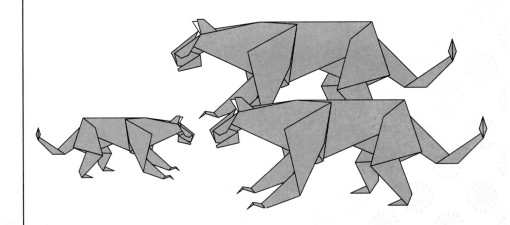

2 Completed Lion.

ZEBRA

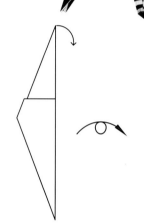

PART I

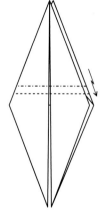

1 Start with Base Fold III. Pleat fold.

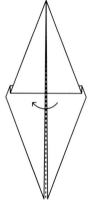

2 Valley fold.

3 Pull and crimp fold as shown, then rotate.

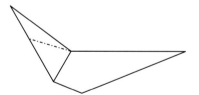

4 Inside reverse fold.

5 Valley fold.

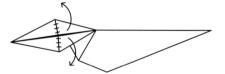

6 Make cuts then valley unfold.

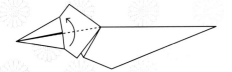

7 Valley fold.

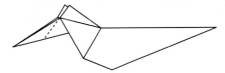

8 Outside reverse fold.

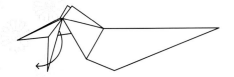

9 Pull some paper out from inside.

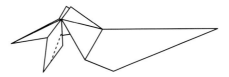

10 Valley folds both front and back.

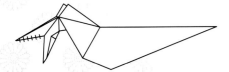

11 Make cut as shown.

12 Valley fold both front and back.

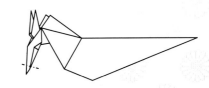

13 Inside reverse fold.

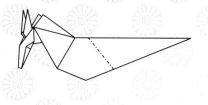

14 Inside reverse fold.

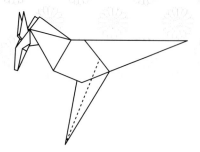

15 Valley folds to both sides.

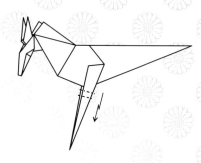

16 Pleat and crimp fold.

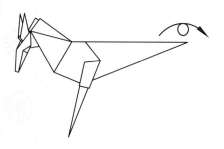

17 Turn over to other side.

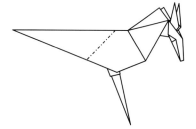

18 Inside reverse fold.

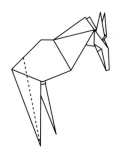

19 Valley folds to both sides.

20 Pleat and crimp.

21 Make cuts into mane, and add pattern.

22 Completed part 1 (front) of zebra.

PART II

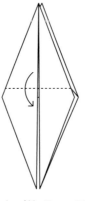

1 Start with Base Fold III.
Valley fold.

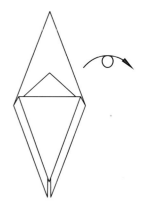

2 Turn over.

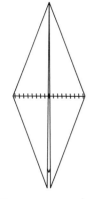

3 Cuts as shown.

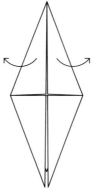

4 Valley folds.

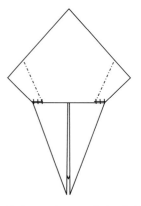

5 Cuts and mountain folds.

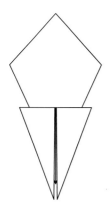

6 Turn over to other side.

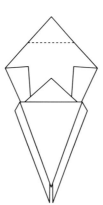

7 Valley fold.

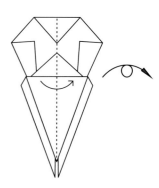

8 Valley fold in half and rotate.

29

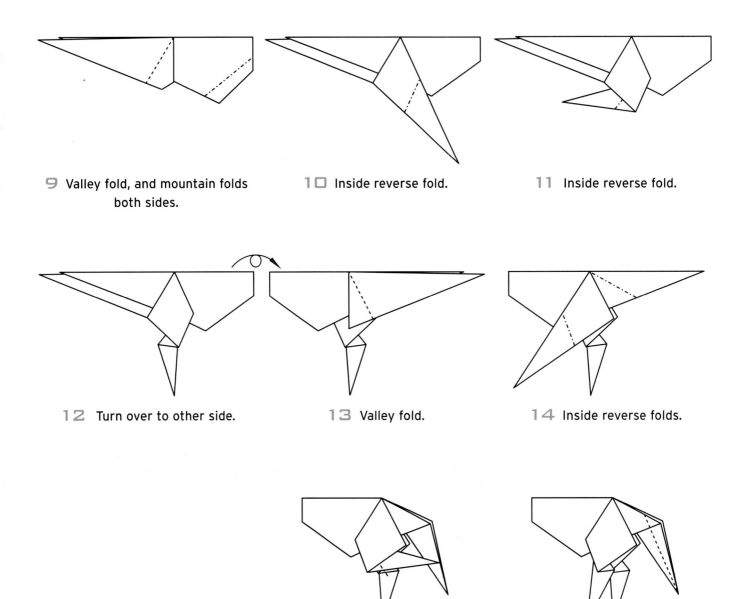

9 Valley fold, and mountain folds both sides.

10 Inside reverse fold.

11 Inside reverse fold.

12 Turn over to other side.

13 Valley fold.

14 Inside reverse folds.

15 Inside reverse fold.

16 Valley fold to both sides.

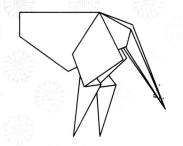

17 Squash fold tail, and add pattern.

18 Completed part 2 (rear) of zebra.

TO ATTACH

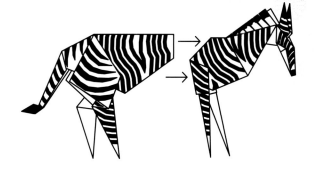

1 Join both parts together and apply glue to hold.

2 Completed Zebra.

DOLPHIN

PART I

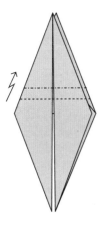

1 Start with Base Fold III. Pleat fold through all layers.

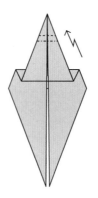

2 Repeat pleat fold through layers.

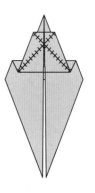

3 Make cuts as shown (to top layer only).

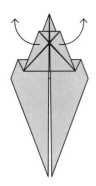

4 Valley folds.

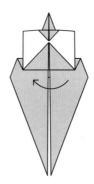

5 Valley fold in half.

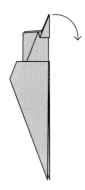

6 Pull and crimp fold.

7 Valley open cut parts.

8 Mountain fold both front and back.

9 Crimp fold.

10 Valley fold both front and back.

11 Valley fold both front and back.

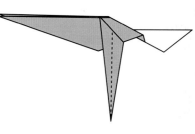

12 Valley fold both sides.

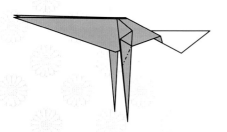

13 Inside reverse folds front and back.

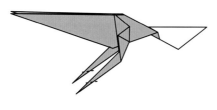

14 Outside reverse folds both sides.

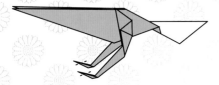

15 Outside reverse folds.

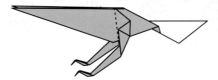

16 Valley folds both front and back.

17 Crimp fold.

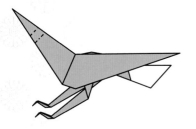

18 Crimp fold.

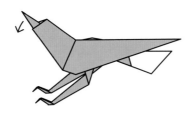

19 Pull into position and squash fold.

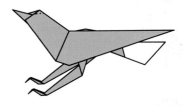

20 Inside reverse fold.

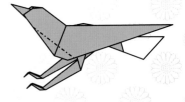

21 Mountain fold both sides.

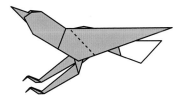

22 Valley fold both sides.

23 Valley fold both sides.

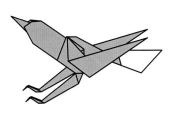

24 Add color and detail.

25 Completed Mockingbird.

CARDINAL

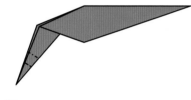

PART I

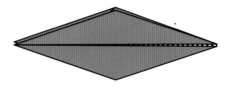

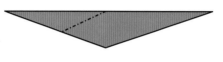

1 Start with Base Fold III. Valley fold in half.

2 Inside reverse fold both flaps together.

3 Crimp fold outer flap only.

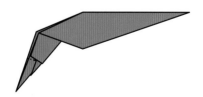

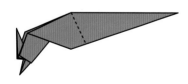

4 Inside reverse fold.

5 Valley fold front and back.

6 Valley fold both sides.

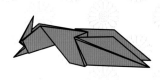

7 Squash fold both sides.

8 Rotate.

9 Completed part 1 of cardinal.

PART II

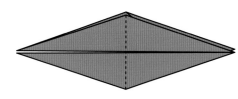

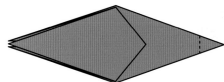

1 Start with Base Fold III. Valley fold top flap to the left.

2 Valley fold.

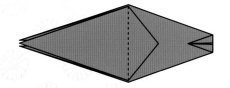

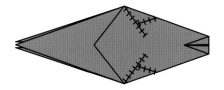

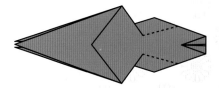

3 Valley fold.

4 Make cuts as shown.

5 Valley fold cut parts.

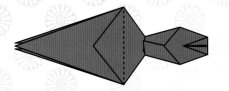

6 Valley fold.

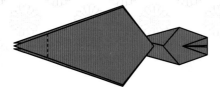

7 Valley fold.

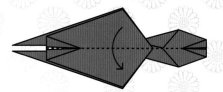

8 Valley fold in half.

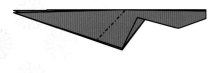

9 Inside reverse fold, both front and back.

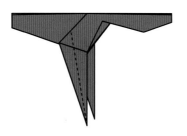

10 Valley fold both sides.

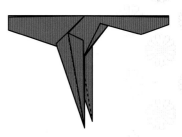

11 Mountain folds.

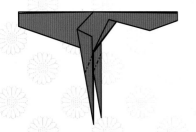

12 Inside reverse fold both sides.

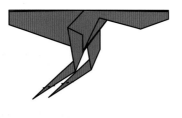

13 Outside reverse folds.

14 Inside reverse fold both sides.

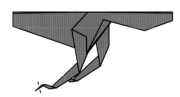

15 Inside reverse fold both sides.

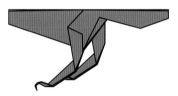

16 Completed part II of Cardinal.

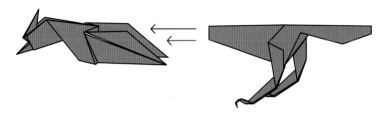

1 Join both parts together as shown and apply glue to hold.

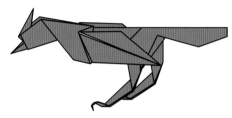

2 Add colors and patterning to completion.

3 Completed Cardinal.

FLYING DRAGON

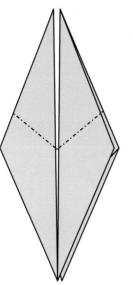

1 Start with Base Fold III. Inside reverse folds.

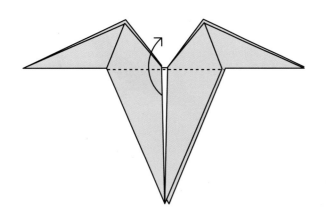

2 Valley fold.

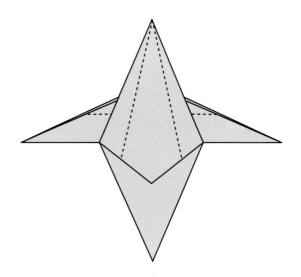

3 Valley folds and squash folds.

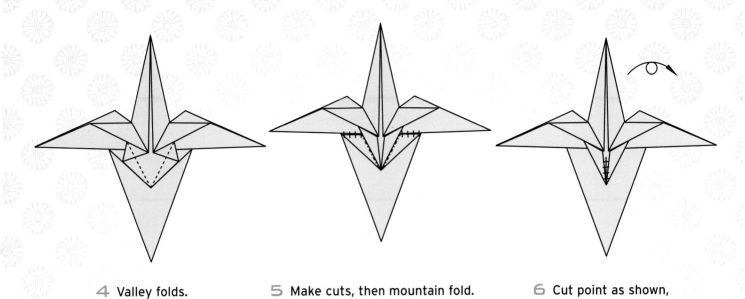

4 Valley folds.

5 Make cuts, then mountain fold.

6 Cut point as shown, then turn to other side.

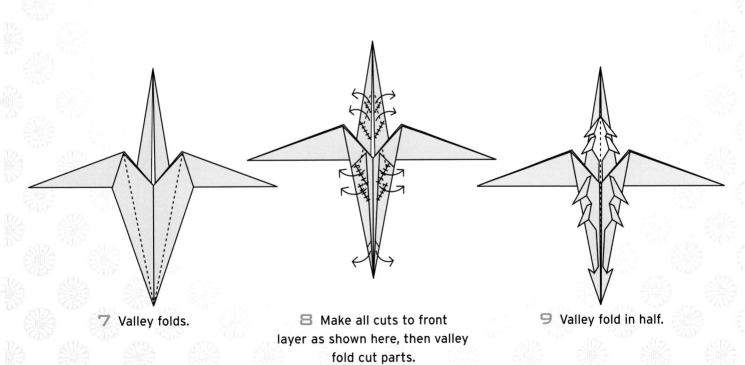

7 Valley folds.

8 Make all cuts to front layer as shown here, then valley fold cut parts.

9 Valley fold in half.

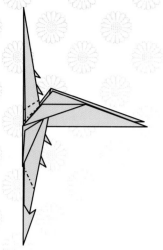

1О Crimp fold, and inside
reverse fold.

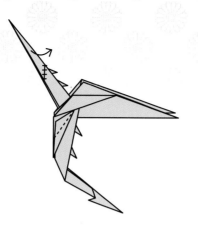

11 Cut and valley unfold. Outside
reverse folds.

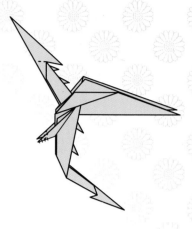

12 Cuts on both folds, then
valley to sides.

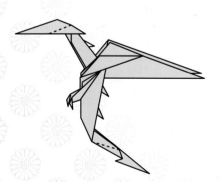

13 Valley folds.

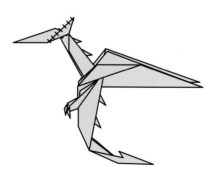

14 Cuts and valley folds.

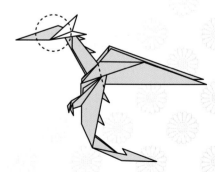

15 Valley folds both sides, then
see close-up views for next steps.

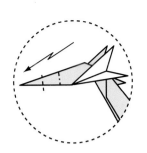

16 Pleat fold.

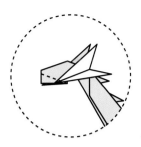

17 Valley fold both sides.

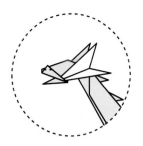

18 Repeat.

19 Back to full view.

20 Mountain folds both sides.

21 Completed Flying Dragon.

UNICORN

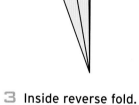

PART I

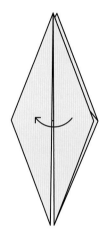

1 Start with Base Fold III. Valley fold in half.

2 Valley fold. Repeat behind.

3 Inside reverse fold.

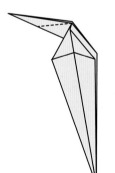

4 Outside reverse fold.

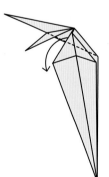

5 Valley fold.

6 Cuts and valley unfolds.

7 Valley fold.

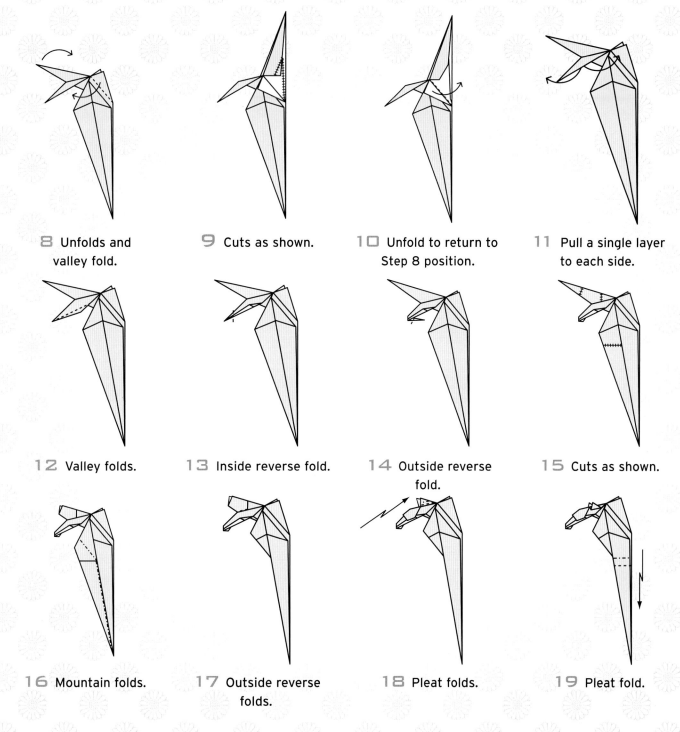

8 Unfolds and valley fold.

9 Cuts as shown.

10 Unfold to return to Step 8 position.

11 Pull a single layer to each side.

12 Valley folds.

13 Inside reverse fold.

14 Outside reverse fold.

15 Cuts as shown.

16 Mountain folds.

17 Outside reverse folds.

18 Pleat folds.

19 Pleat fold.

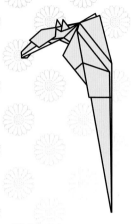

20 Tuck both side flaps inside.

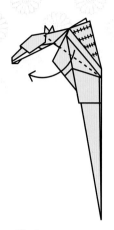

21 Cuts and valley fold.

22 Valley fold.

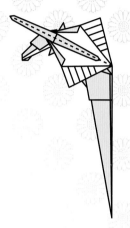

23 Valley fold.

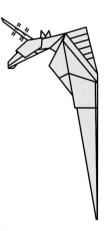

24 Crimp folds.

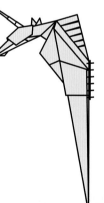

25 Cut edge as shown.

26 Completed part 1 of unicorn.

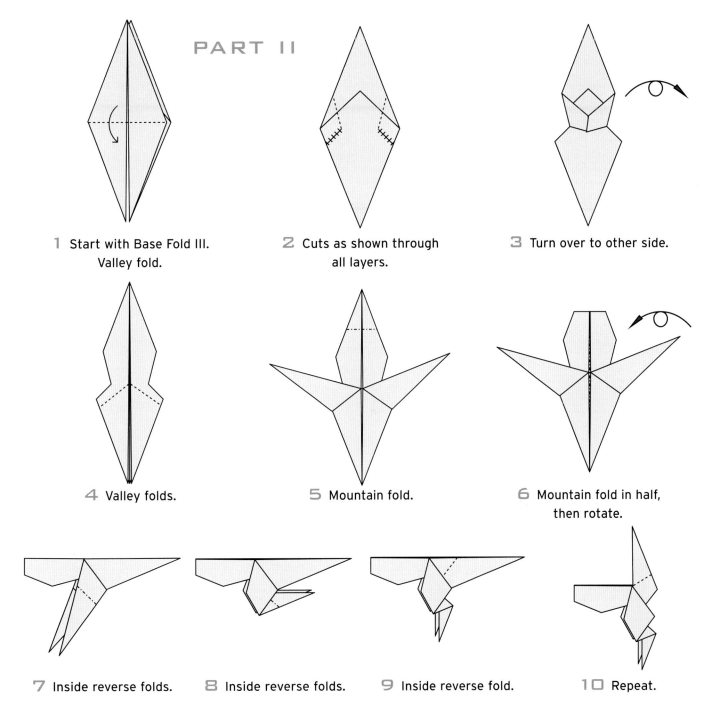

PART II

1 Start with Base Fold III.
Valley fold.

2 Cuts as shown through
all layers.

3 Turn over to other side.

4 Valley folds.

5 Mountain fold.

6 Mountain fold in half,
then rotate.

7 Inside reverse folds.

8 Inside reverse folds.

9 Inside reverse fold.

10 Repeat.

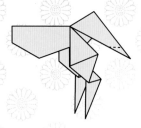

11 Outside reverse fold.

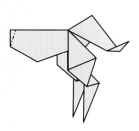

12 Inside reverse fold.

13 Completed part 2 of unicorn.

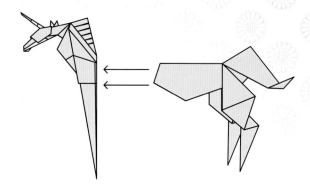

1 Join both parts together. Apply glue to hold and separate legs for standing.

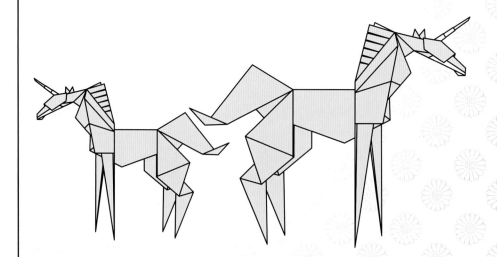

2 Completed Unicorn.

INTRODUCTION TO ORIGAMI TESSELLATIONS

ORIGAMI IS USUALLY used to create animals or other figures, as in the earlier projects in this book. Origami can also be used to create boxes and other geometric figures that many people find beautiful by virtue of their symmetry. The remainder of this book will be concerned with origami tessellations, a particular type of geometric figure.

A tessellation is a collection of shapes that fit together without gaps or overlaps to cover the mathematical plane. Another word for tessellation is tiling, and the shapes in a tessellation are the individual tiles, just like with floor tiles. In recent years, creating tessellations by paper folding has been a growing segment of the origami landscape, allowing the creation of beautiful and fascinating geometric objects.

Since an origami piece is folded from a finite piece of paper, origami tessellations are actually small portions of a design that could in principal be extended without end. Five origami projects are described in the following pages.

There are three "regular" tessellations, in which each shape is the same type and size of regular polygon. These are shown in the following illustration; all three will figure in your origami tessellation projects.

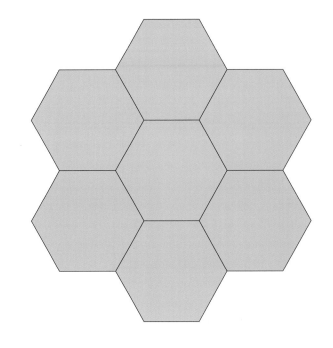

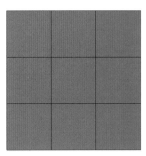

BASIC GRIDS

IN EACH OF THESE PROJECTS, the first step is to crease the paper to create the geometric grid on which the particular piece is based. This process is a bit tedious, but it is necessary and needs to be carried out accurately. To help guide you, the grids are printed as light gray lines on special sheets in your kit provided for these projects.

Some of the projects have six-fold symmetry. In these cases, the finished project will be more symmetric if the starting sheet also has six-fold symmetry. For this reason, an overall hexagon boundary is indicated for you to cut out prior to folding on some of the sheets. In addition, mountain and valley folds are also indicated on the printed sheets, with heavy red and blue lines, respectively.

After folding these projects using the marked sheets, you may want to try folding them using unmarked sheets. The grids can also be created using an unmarked square of paper. In the case of a square grid, simply fold the sheet in half in each direction, use these crease lines to guide folding in quarters, eighths, etc. as necessary.

To create a grid of equilateral triangles:

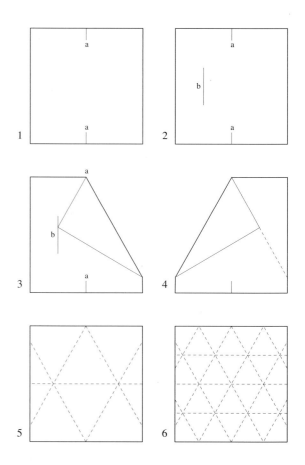

1. Book fold the sheet to create creases at the ends of a centerline.

2. Valley fold to crease "a" to obtain crease "b" $1/4$ of the way across the sheet.

3. Fold a corner to crease "b", using crease "a" as a guide point.

4. Fold the opposing corner, using the crease just created as a guide.

5. Rotate the sheet 180° and repeat steps 3 and 4. Then fold the sheet in half top to bottom.

6. Fold in quarters top to bottom. Then use the intersections of the crease lines to guide folding of additional diagonal creases. Repeat this step for eighths, sixteenths, etc. as necessary.

CHECKERBOARD SQUARES

THIS FIRST PROJECT results in raised black squares against a background of white squares. The geometric tessellation is the simplest possible, the squares pattern shown on page 65. When you're finished, the flipside will be a woven pattern of larger squares. This sort of tessellation of squares is one of the most basic origami tessellations, and a number of people have worked on variants of this. One of the earliest people to work on this sort of origami tessellation is Shuzo Fujimoto, but the same basic design can be seen in quilts that predate origami tessellations by decades.

For an origami tessellation that is periodic, or repeating, any number of repeat units can be formed. This project will form 9 raised squares (3x3), but you could also form 16 (4x4), 25 (5x5), or even more. To do so, you would need to form a denser crease grid and work on a finer scale, or use a larger sheet of paper.

With origami tessellations, the polygons that stand out in the final piece usually need to be laid flat using a twisting motion. This takes some getting used to, but is probably easiest to accomplish using squares. This project will introduce you to this idea.

1 With the printed side face up, form valley-fold creases along all of the grid lines running parallel to the paper edges (both horizontally and vertically).
2 Flip the sheet over and form mountain-fold creases along all of the grid lines running diagonally across the paper.
3 Form mountain folds around the central square.

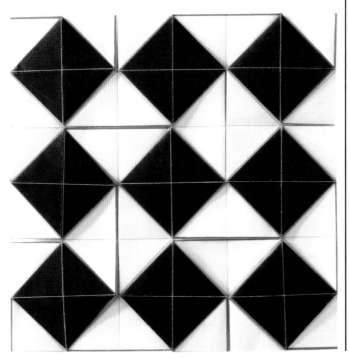

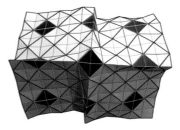

4 Begin folding the four mountain folds and the four valley folds radiating from the central squares. This will cause the central square to buckle.

5 Continue the buckling process until the center square is folded in half. All four of the mountain folds radiating outward from the square are folded now, but two of the valley folds are folded and two are flat.

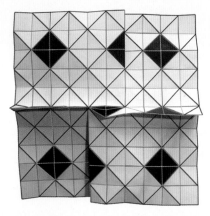

6 Fold the remaining two valley folds, so that there is a central ridge running from left to right.

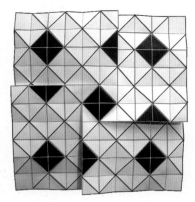

7 Lay the two halves of this ridge flat, to obtain a flat piece in which the center square sits up higher than the surrounding paper.

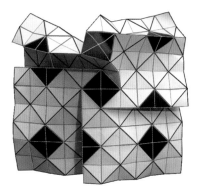

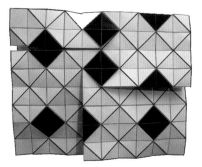

8 Fold the valley and mountain folds radiating outward from the square immediately above the center square, so that the square twists (counterclockwise) down flat. Repeat this process with the squares to the right and left of the center square, as well as the square below. These squares will all twist counterclockwise.

9 Fold the square on the opposite side of the center square in the same fashion.

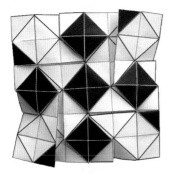

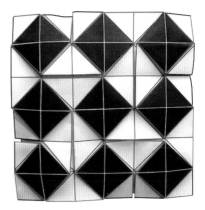

1 0 Fold the remaining two squares closest to the center square in the same fashion.

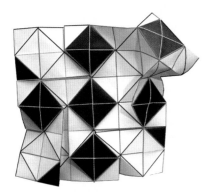

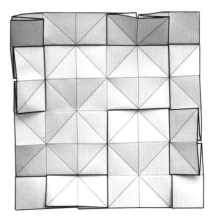

1 1 Fold one of the corner squares in a similar fashion. Partially open up the piece in the vicinity of the square and then perform the indicated mountain and valley folds, causing it to twist down into place. In contrast to the squares you just completed, these corner squares will twist clockwise.

1 2 Fold the remaining three squares in the same fashion. The finished piece is shown in one illustration, while the other illustration shows the flipside of the finished piece—a weave of larger squares.

DANCING SQUARES

THIS PROJECT RESULTS in 16 raised squares against a background of triangles. The squares have two different orientations, which gives them a sense of motion. As you fold this, you will notice that it is closely related to the Checkerboard Squares tessellation.

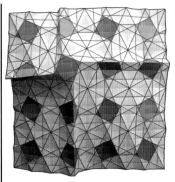

3 Fold one of the center 4 squares; the start of this process is shown in the first illustration. It helps to mountain fold the red lines radiating outward from the square. The square will twist as it lays down. The blue squares will rotate counterclockwise as they twist, and the green ones will rotate clockwise.

4 Fold one of the two adjacent squares in a similar manner. You will need to partially unfold the paper around the square first.

1 With the printed side up, form valley-fold creases along all of the grid lines running parallel to the paper edges (both horizontally and vertically).

2 Form mountain-fold creases along all of the grid lines running diagonally across the paper.

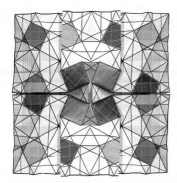

5 Fold the other two squares in the center group of four. In order to get them to twist down smoothly, be sure all the creases start bending correctly.

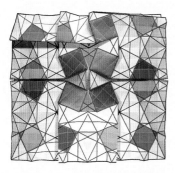

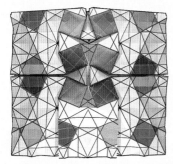

6 Fold one of the eight squares closest to the central four in a similar manner. Then fold the one next to it.

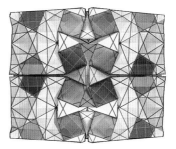

7 Continue to fold the opposing pair of squares in the same manner. Then fold the remaining four adjacent to the central four.

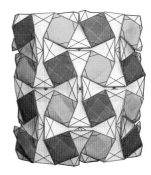

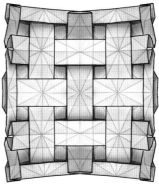

8 Finally, fold the four squares near the corners of the sheet. The backside of the finished project will exhibit a weave pattern.

STELLAR HEXAGON

THIS PROJECT FORMS a geometric object that cannot directly be repeated to cover the infinite plane, so strictly speaking it might not be called an origami tessellation. However, it could potentially form a building block in a tessellation. A wide variety of tessellations incorporate hexagons and hexagonal stars. This folding was discovered by Eric Gjerde.

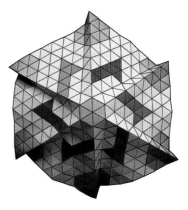

4 Begin folding the mountain and valley folds radiating outward from the small central hexagon.

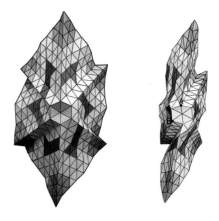

1 Cut out the overall hexagon.
2 With the printed side face up, form valley-fold creases along all of the grid lines.
3 Also perform mountain folds on those grid lines with red lines on them.

5 Bring the sides in, pushing the top and bottom folds toward the center, so that the central hexagon begins to buckle as shown.

72

6 Continue folding so that the paper twists, bringing point A to point B. The paper will now lay flat as shown, folded in half.

7 Open up the paper to lay the full hexagon flat, with a ridge standing up in the center. Flatten out the two halves of the ridge.

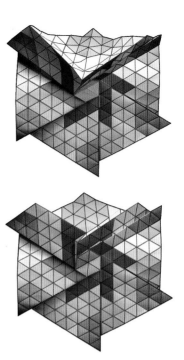

8 Fold any one of the six regions where red and blue areas meet. First, partially open up the paper, and then refold following the indicated mountain and valley fold lines.

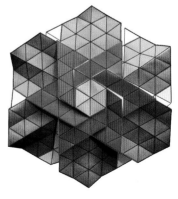

9 Fold the other five analogous regions in a similar fashion.

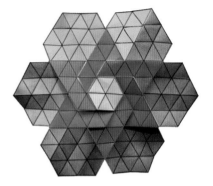

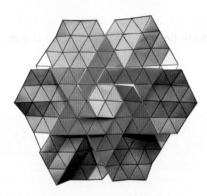

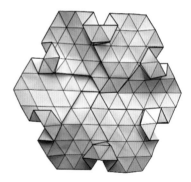

1O Fold one of the six remaining areas. First open the folds, then refold the region so that all of the valley folds go the correct way. This results in a sort of pyramid as shown in the center illustration. Finally, fold everything down flat by making one side of this region tuck behind the other.

11 Fold the other five remaining areas in the same manner, to achieve the finished project.

TRIPLE-TIERED HEXAGONS

THIS PROJECT FORMS rings of hexagons arranged around a central hexagon, with each successive ring on a lower tier. It can be made as large as desired. The flipside of the finished project is a regular tessellation of hexagons like that shown on page 65. This folding was also dicovered by Eric Gjerde.

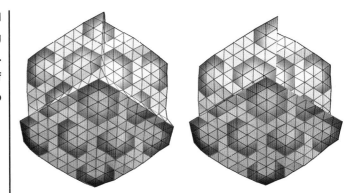

4 Begin forming ridges by folding the mountain and valley folds radiating outward from one of the small triangles at a corner of the central hexagon. Fold these three ridges down flat according to the mountain and valley folds indicated.

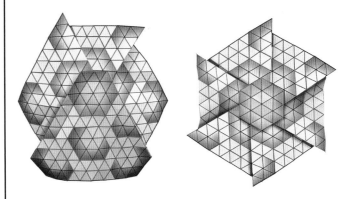

1 Cut out the overall hexagon.
2 With the printed side face up, form valley-fold creases along all of the grid lines.
3 Also perform mountain folds on those grid lines with red lines on them.

5 Fold the regions at the other five corners of the central hexagon in the same manner.

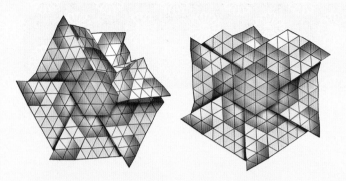

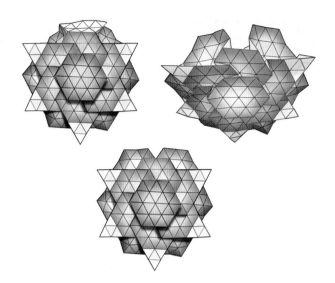

6 Fold any one of the six unfolded regions nearest to the central hexagon. First, partially open up the project in that region, and then fold it back down flat according to the lines indicating mountain and valley folds.

8 Fold one of the six areas at the tips of the six-pointed star. First, partially open up the project as shown in the first illustration, then begin to fold according to the indicated blue and red lines, as shown in the next illustration, until it lays flat.

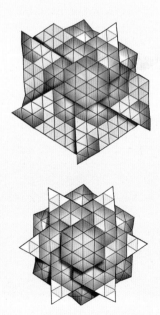

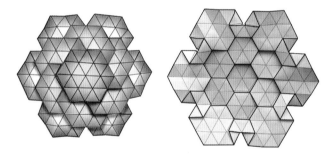

7 Fold the remaining five regions of this sort.

9 Fold the other five regions of this type to complete the project. If this origami tessellation is extended by using larger paper or a smaller grid, the regular hexagon tessellation in the central portion of the flipside will continue outward.

TRIANGLE SQUASH

THIS PROJECT FORMS an array of small triangles on the front side. The flipside of the finished project is a regular tessellation of hexagons, but larger ones than those for the preceding project. This tessellation can be made as large as desired. This folding was also discovered by Eric Gjerde.

1 Cut out the overall hexagon.
2 With the printed side face up, form valley-fold creases along all of the grid lines parallel to the edges of the large hexagon.
3 For those creases that have red lines along them, also perform mountain folds.
4 Form mountain folds on the grid lines that are not parallel to the edges of the overall hexagon. These all lie along edges of the small yellow and orange triangles.

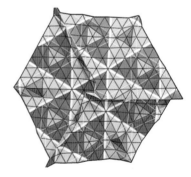

5 Form three ridges radiating outward from the small triangle in the center of the paper. This will leave a collapsed triangle sticking up in irregular fashion. The ridges should fold downward along the blue valley lines.

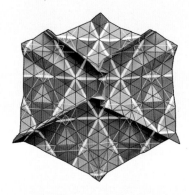

6 Raise up one of the three adjacent triangles by forming two more ridges.

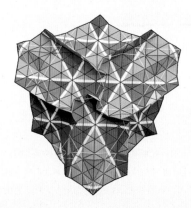

7 Raise up the other two adjacent triangles. The ridges will be a little chaotic between the triangles.

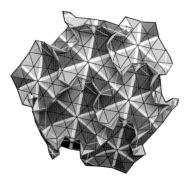

8 Carry out this process for the remaining nine triangles. At this point, the project should look something like the illustration. The flipside should now look very much like the flipside of the finished project (a regular tessellation of hexagons).

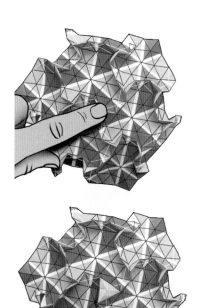

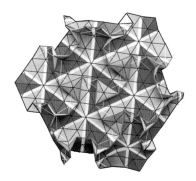

1□ Carry out this same flattening process for the three triangles adjacent to the center triangle.

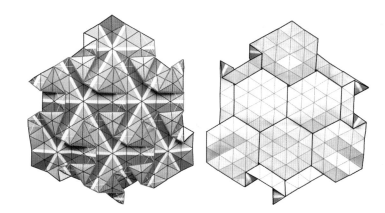

9 Now comes the fun part: squashing the triangles! Be sure all three arms of the center triangle are standing up uniformly, as shown in the illustration in the previous step. Place your fingertip on the center of this triangle and push down firmly. The triangle will suddenly "pop" flat.

11 Flatten the remaining nine triangles in the same manner, resulting in the finished project. You may want to hold the finished project up to the light, as the light-and-dark pattern resulting from the light passing through single versus tripled-over portions of the paper will give the piece a different look.

INDEX

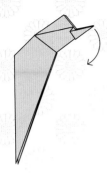

7 Pull and crimp fold.

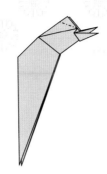

8 Mountain fold.

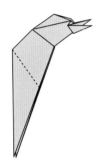

9 Valley folds.

10 Mountain fold both sides.

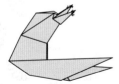

11 Cuts as shown.

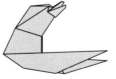

12 Completed part 1 of dolphin.

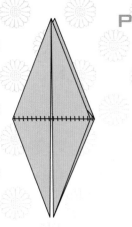

1 Start with Base Fold III.
  Cut as shown.

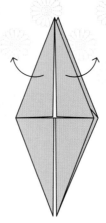

2 Valley folds.

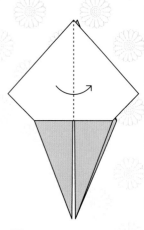

3 Valley fold in half.

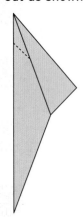

4 Outside reverse fold.

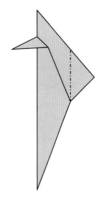

5 Mountain fold.

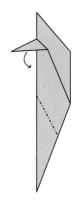

6 Pull paper outward at top;
  mountain fold below.

7 Outside reverse at top.
  Mountain fold below.

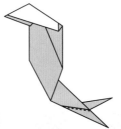

8 Valley fold and glue
  into position.

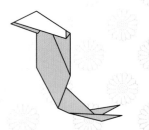

9 Completed part 2 of dolphin.

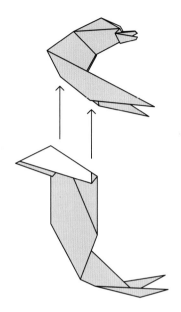

1 Join both parts together as shown.

2 Valley fold both sides.

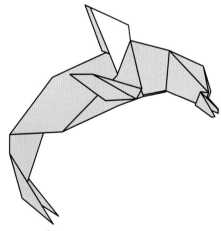

3 Completed Dolphin.

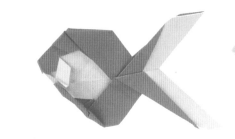

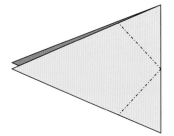

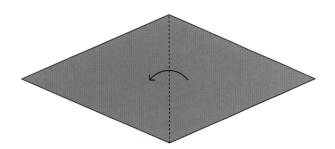

1 Valley fold in half.

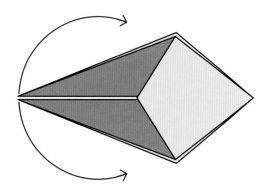

2 Inside reverse folds.

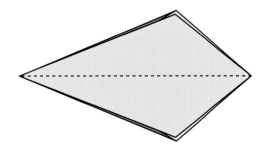

3 Valley fold both front and back.

4 Inside reverse folds.

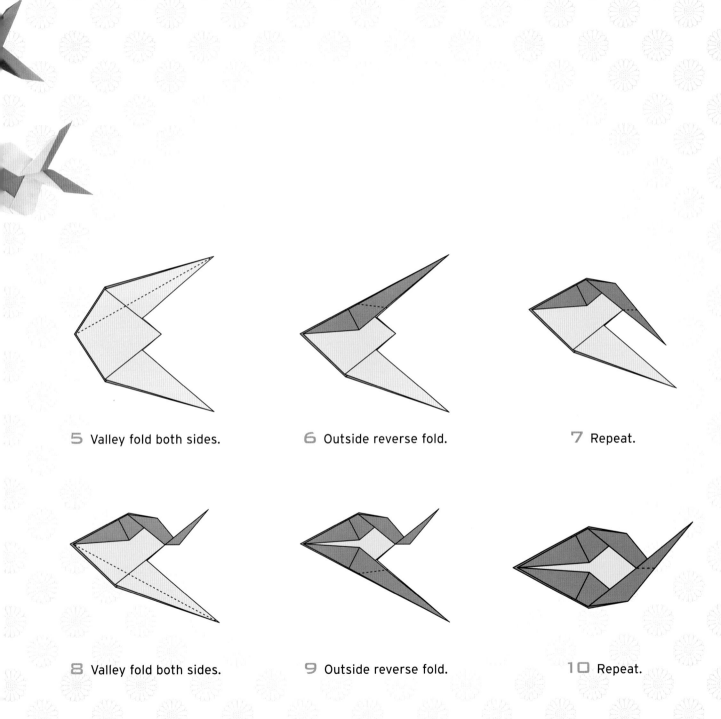

5 Valley fold both sides.

6 Outside reverse fold.

7 Repeat.

8 Valley fold both sides.

9 Outside reverse fold.

10 Repeat.

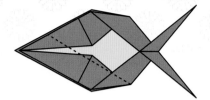

11 Valley fold layer to front.

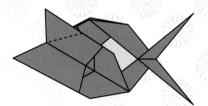

12 Valley fold.

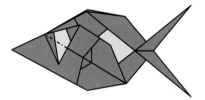

13 Mountain fold to inside.

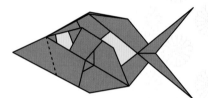

14 Valley fold.

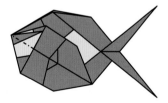

15 Mountain fold to inside.

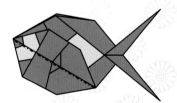

16 Mountain fold to back.

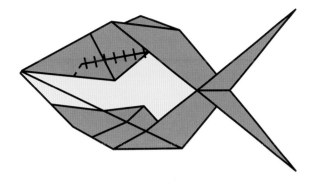

17 Cuts and valley out to sides both front and back.

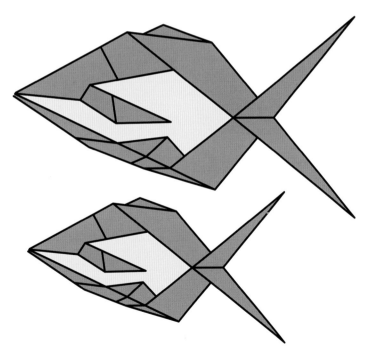

18 Completed Coral Fish.

KILLER WHALE

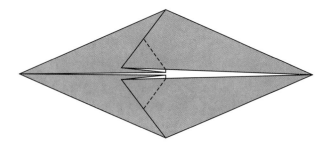

1 Start with Base Fold I, then valley folds.

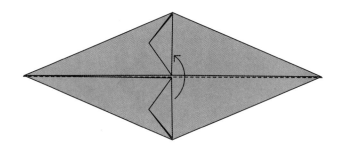

2 Valley fold in half.

3 Inside reverse fold, as shown.

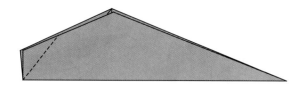

4 Valley folds front and back.

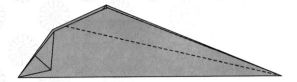

5 Valley folds front and back.

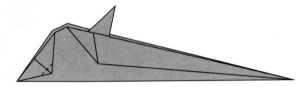

6 Valley folds front and back for "eyes."

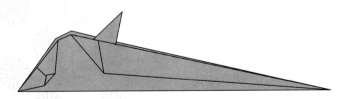

7 Completed part 1 (top) of killer whale.

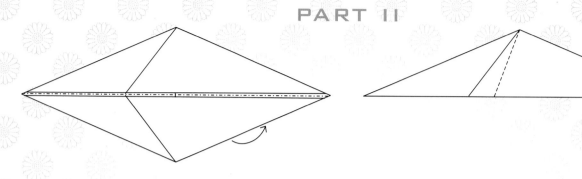

PART II

1 Start with Base Fold I, then mountain fold in half.

2 Valley folds both sides.

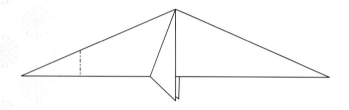

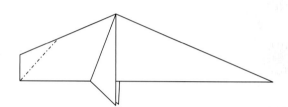

3 Inside reverse fold.

4 Mountain folds front and back.

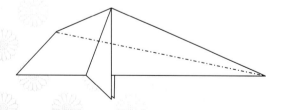

5 Mountain folds front and back.

6 Completed part 2 (bottom) of killer whale.

TO ATTACH

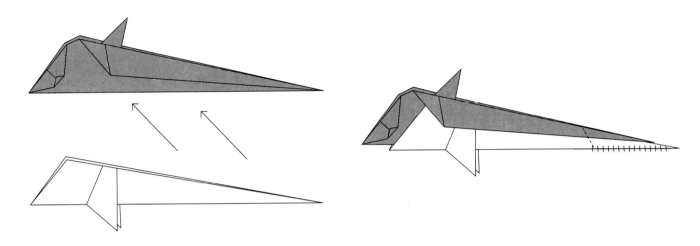

1 Put parts 1 and 2 together, as shown, and glue front body part to hold.

2 Cut through layers as indicated, lightly valley fold "tail fin" layers front and back to separate.

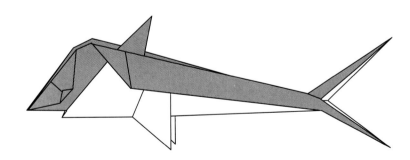

3 Completed Killer Whale.

PENGUIN

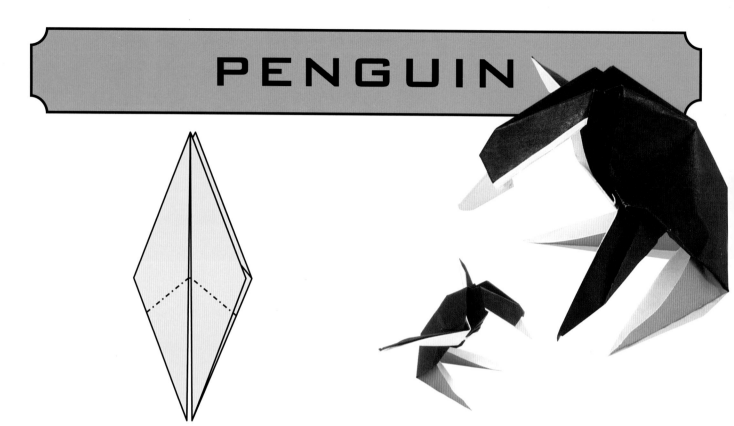

1 Start with Base Fold III. Inside reverse folds.

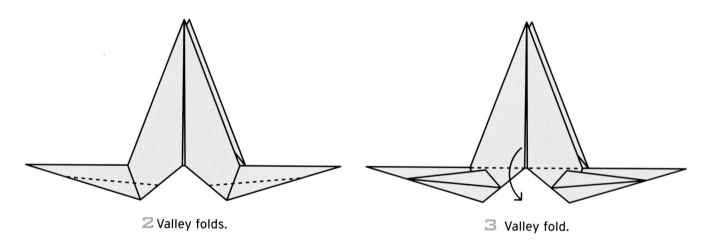

2 Valley folds.

3 Valley fold.

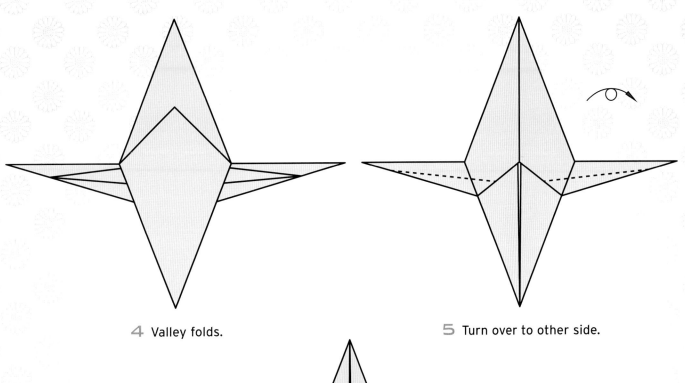

4 Valley folds.

5 Turn over to other side.

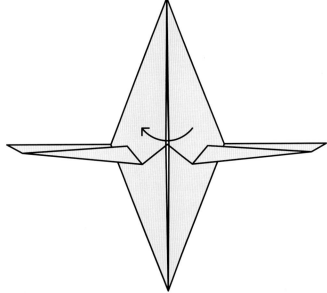

6 Valley fold in half.

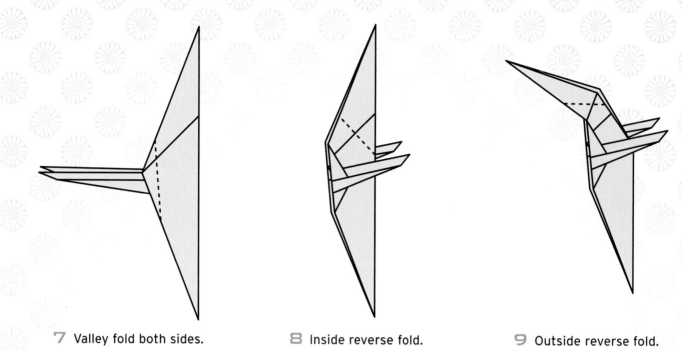

7 Valley fold both sides.　　**8** Inside reverse fold.　　**9** Outside reverse fold.

46

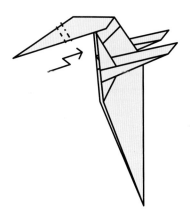

10 Pleat fold.

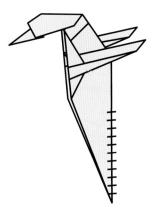

11 Cut as shown.

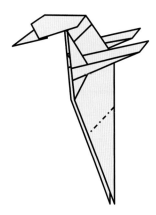

12 Mountain fold both sides.

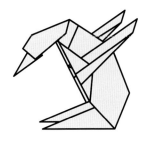

13 Add coloring if you wish.

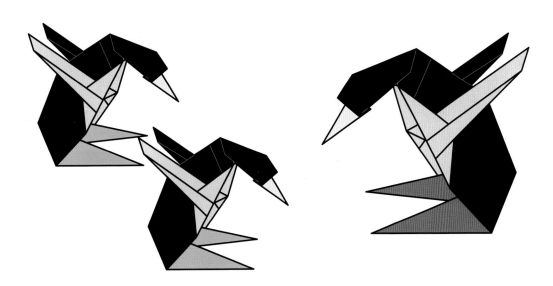

14 Completed Penguin.

47

MOCKINGBIRD

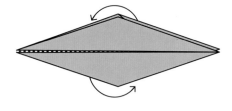

1 Start with Base Fold III. Valley fold both sides.

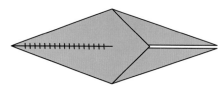

2 Cut as shown on both sides.

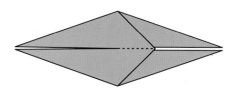

3 Valley folds to return to step 1 position.

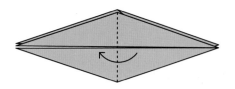

4 Valley fold top layer.

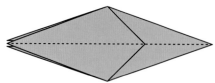

5 Valley fold in half.

6 Cut top layers front and back.